making math visual activity book

Grades K - 1

Addition and Subtraction Games and Activities

created by
Colleen Uscianowski, PhD
edited by
Marshall Maa

LUMINOUSLEARNING   www.luminouslearning.com

10 9 8 7 6 5 4 3 2

Published by Luminous Learning Inc, New York
Orders: www.luminouslearning.com
info@luminouslearning.com

ISBN 978-1-939763-08-2

Visit us online: **www.luminouslearning.com**

Let's Connect!

f facebook.com/LuminousLearning

twitter.com/luminouslearn

youtube.com/user/Luminouslearning

pinterest.com/luminouslearn

www.instagram.com/luminouslearning

LUMINOUSLEARNING

making math visual activity book
Grades K - 1 Addition and Subtraction Games and Activities

Table of Contents

Game materials: The math games and activities in this book help children to practice addition and subtraction using number lines and unifix cubes (also called connecting cubes or linking cubes). *If you do not have a set of unifix cubes, you can use other math manipulatives.* For example, you can use square tiles or counters, such as beans or buttons. In addition, you can cut out and use the square tiles in the appendix to play the games that require unifix cubes.

LUMINOUSLEARNING   www.luminouslearning.com

Climb to 10

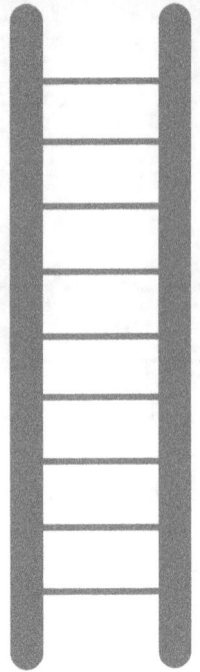

PLAYERS

2 players

MATERIALS

- *Climb to 10 gameboard.* Two students share the same gameboard, which helps them to compare their numbers and see which player is closer to reaching 10. You can laminate the gameboard so that it lasts longer.
- *Addition cards.* Use the provided addition cards. Print them on thick paper so that students cannot see through the cards. Cut out each card along the dotted lines. You can laminate the addition cards so that they last longer.
- *Unifix cubes.* Each set of players should have a basket of unifix cubes (each student will need 10 in total). Students will use the unifix cubes to create a chain of 10 cubes.

DIRECTIONS

1. Shuffle the addition cards and place them face down in front of the pair of students.
2. Every player starts with zero unifix cubes.
3. Player one pulls an addition card from the top of the pile. The card will tell the student how many unifix cubes to add. The student should read the card aloud and add that many unifix cubes to their ladder. For example, if they pull a card that says "+2" on the first round, the student stacks 2 unifix cubes together and lays it down on their ladder.
4. Player two pulls an addition card from the top of the pile and repeats step 3 above.
5. The players continue to take turns turning over addition cards and adding unifix cubes to their stack. The first player to make it to 10 wins!

Climb to 10

PLAYER ONE

10
9
8
7
6
5
4
3
2
1

PLAYER TWO

10
9
8
7
6
5
4
3
2
1

Addition Cards

+0

+0

+0

+1

Addition Cards

+1

+1

+1

+1

Addition Cards

+ 1

+ 1

+ 1

+ 2

Addition Cards

+2

+2

+2

+2

Addition Cards

+ 2

+ 2

+ 2

+ 2

How many more?

SMALL GROUP ACTIVITY

1- 6 students

MATERIALS

- *How many more* 10-frame cards. Cut each page in half to create 20 cards. If you are working with more than two students, you should duplicate the set of cards to create more. You can photocopy the cards on cardstock and laminate them to make them last longer.
- *Unifix cubes.* Each student should have a basket of unifix cubes. Students will place the unifix cubes in the 10-frame on the cards to find out how many more they need to equal ten.
- *Dry erase marker* (optional). If you laminate the cards, students can use a dry erase marker to fill in the equation when they determine the missing number of unifix cubes.

DIRECTIONS

1. The student takes a card and fills in the 10-frame with the missing number of unifix cubes. For example, if the card reads $3 + \boxed{} = 10$, the student should fill the 10-frame with 7 additional unifix cubes because $3 + 7 = 10$.
2. If the cards are laminated, the student can fill in the missing addend in the equation using a dry erase marker. Otherwise, they can write in the missing addend using a pencil.
3. The student continues taking cards and repeats steps 1 - 2.
4. **To turn *How Many More?* into a game:** Students can work in pairs or a small group. They each turn over a card and fill in the 10-frame with the missing number of unifix cubes. After each round, each student keeps the number of unifix cubes they used to fill in the 10-frame. When they have gone through every card, students count up the number of unifix cubes they used in total. The student with the highest number of unifix cubes wins!

How many more cubes do you need to make 10?

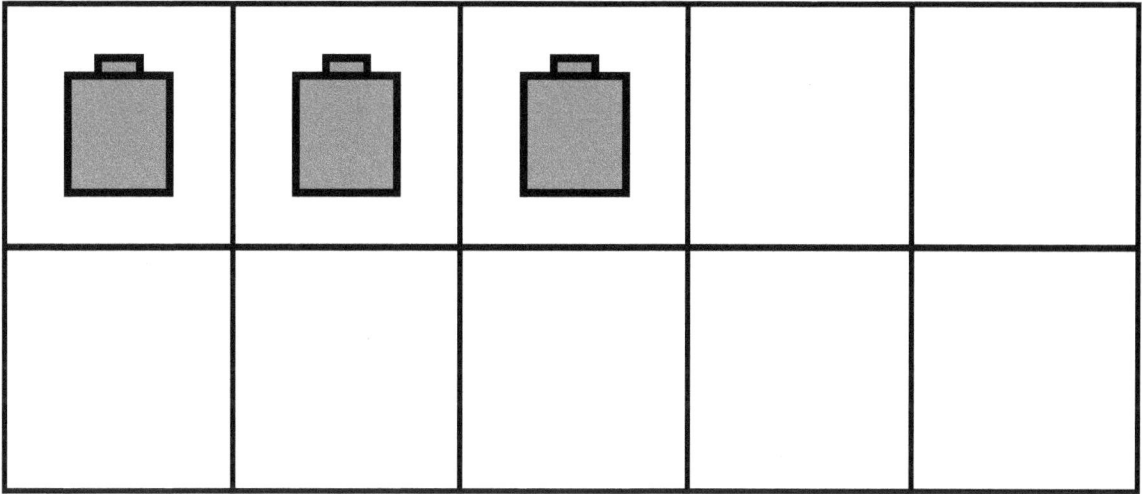

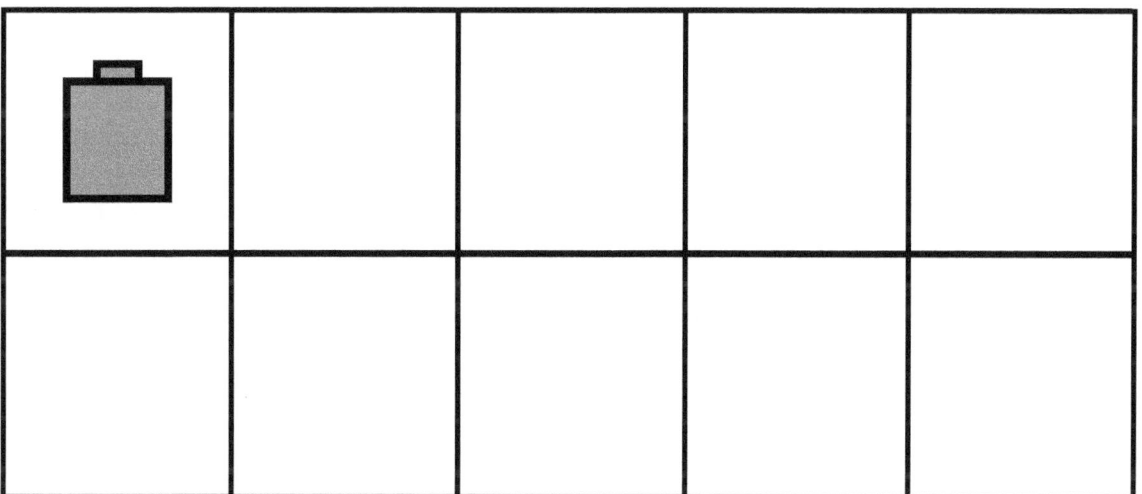

$$3 + \boxed{} = 10$$

- -

How many more cubes do you need to make 10?

$$1 + \boxed{} = 10$$

How many more cubes do you need to make 10?

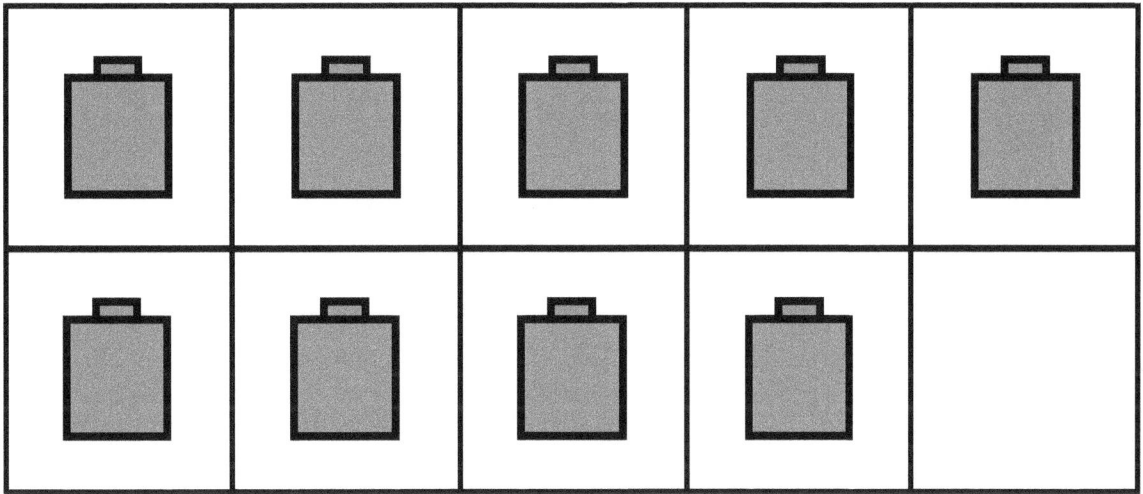

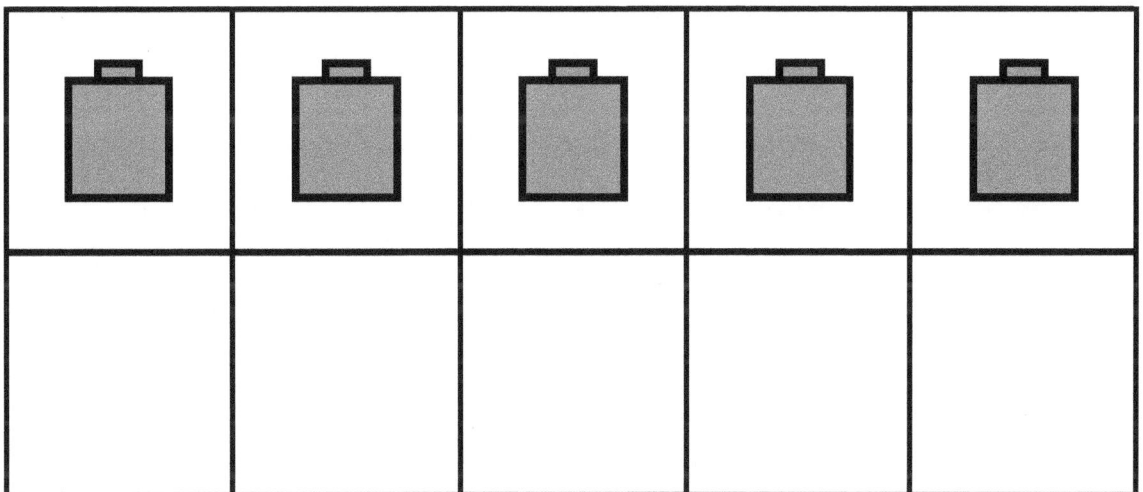

$$9 + \boxed{} = 10$$

- -

How many more cubes do you need to make 10?

$$5 + \boxed{} = 10$$

How many more cubes do you need to make 10?

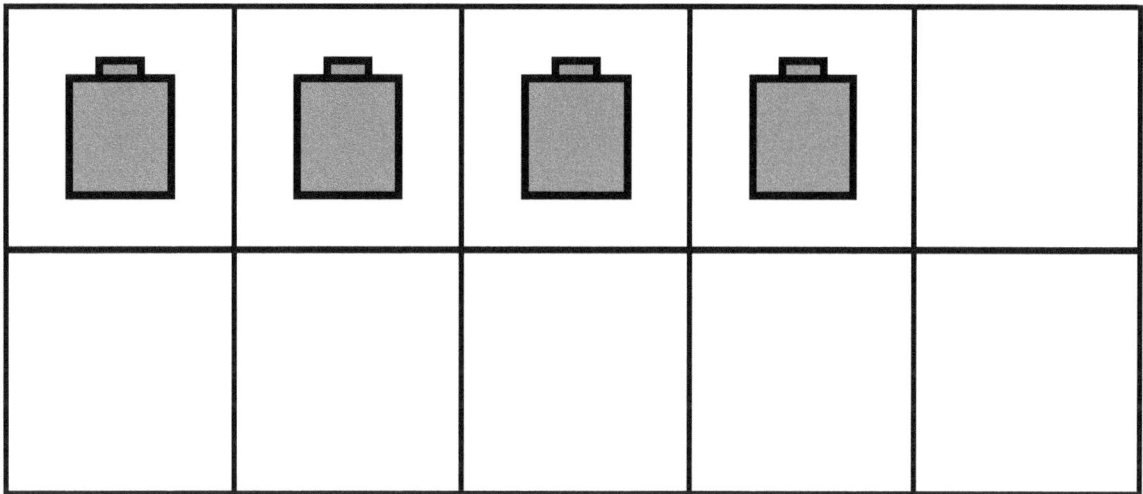

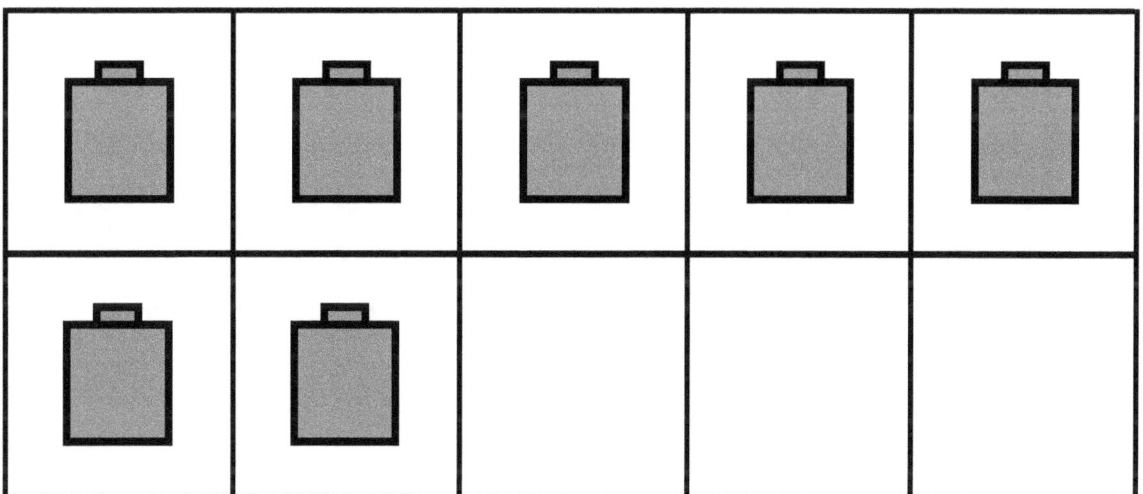

$4 + \boxed{} = 10$

How many more cubes do you need to make 10?

$7 + \boxed{} = 10$

How many more cubes do you need to make 10?

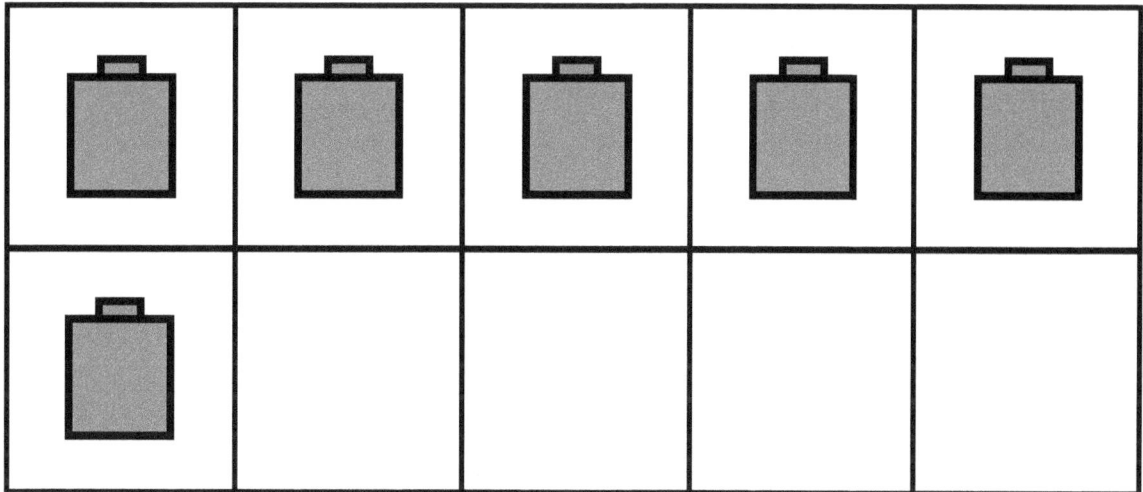

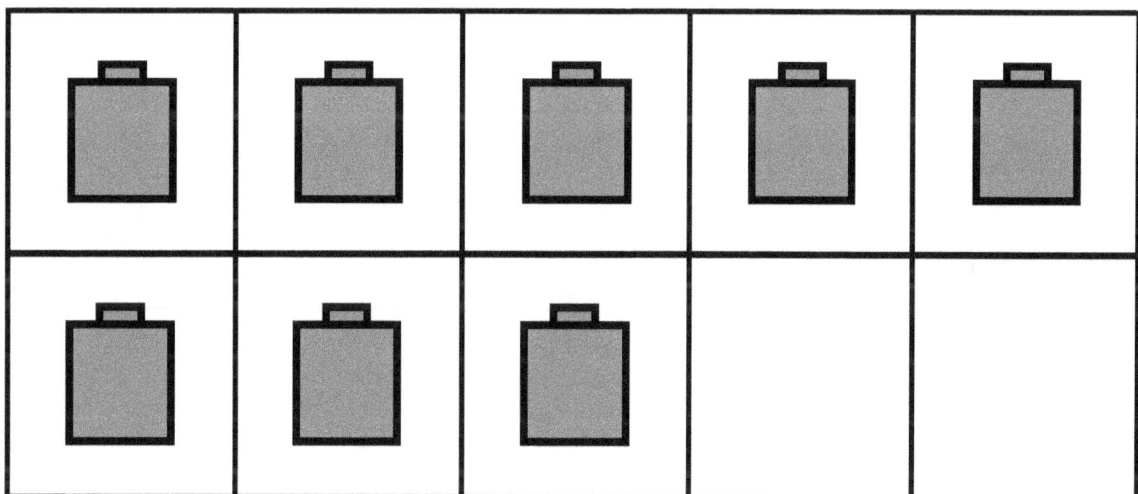

$$6 + \boxed{} = 10$$

- -

How many more cubes do you need to make 10?

$$8 + \boxed{} = 10$$

How many more cubes do you need to make 10?

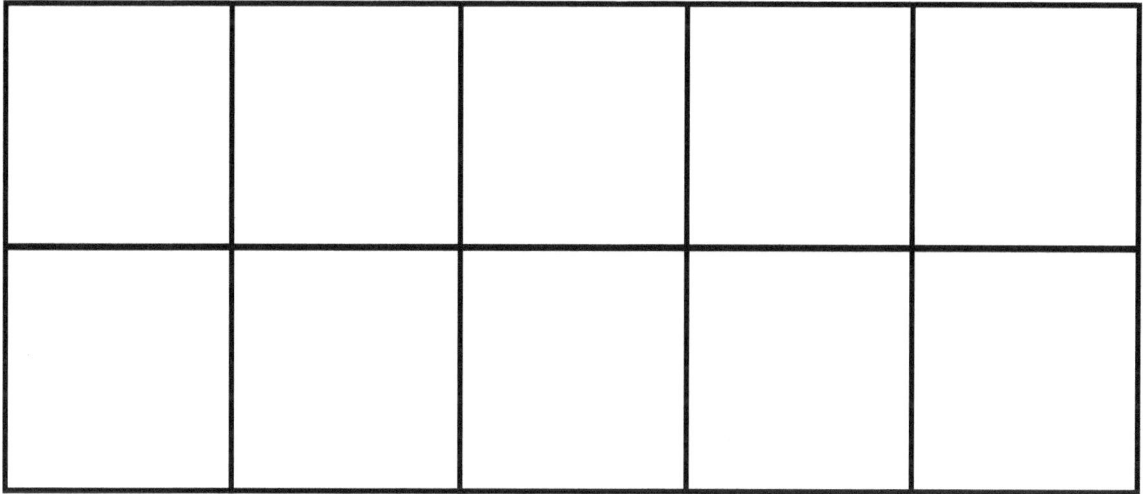

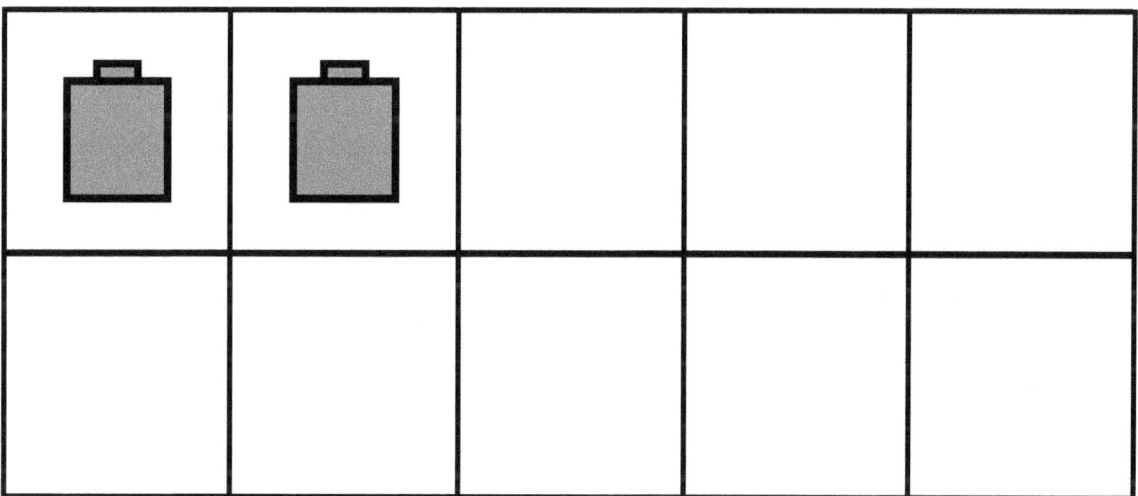

$$0 + \boxed{} = 10$$

- -

How many more cubes do you need to make 10?

$$2 + \boxed{} = 10$$

How many more cubes do you need to make 10?

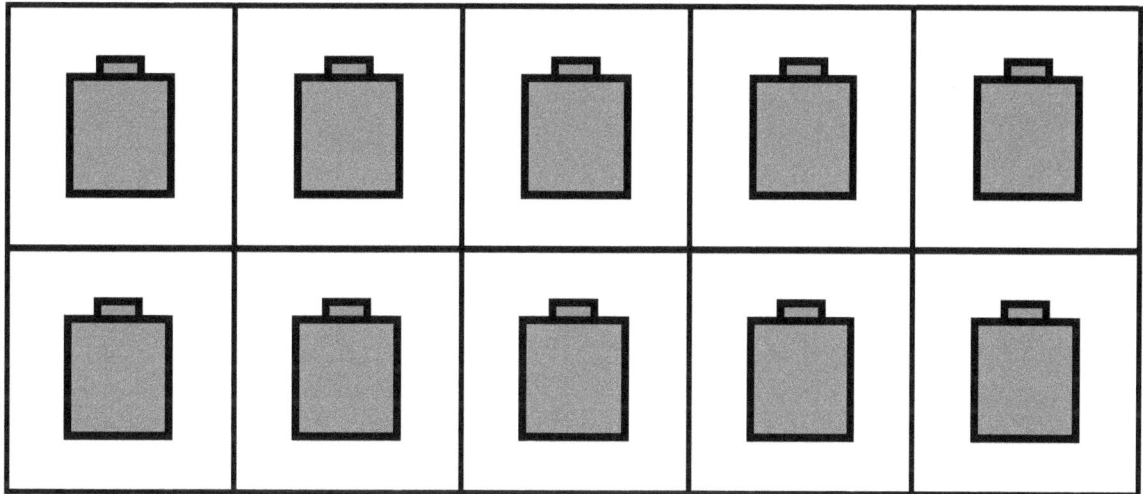

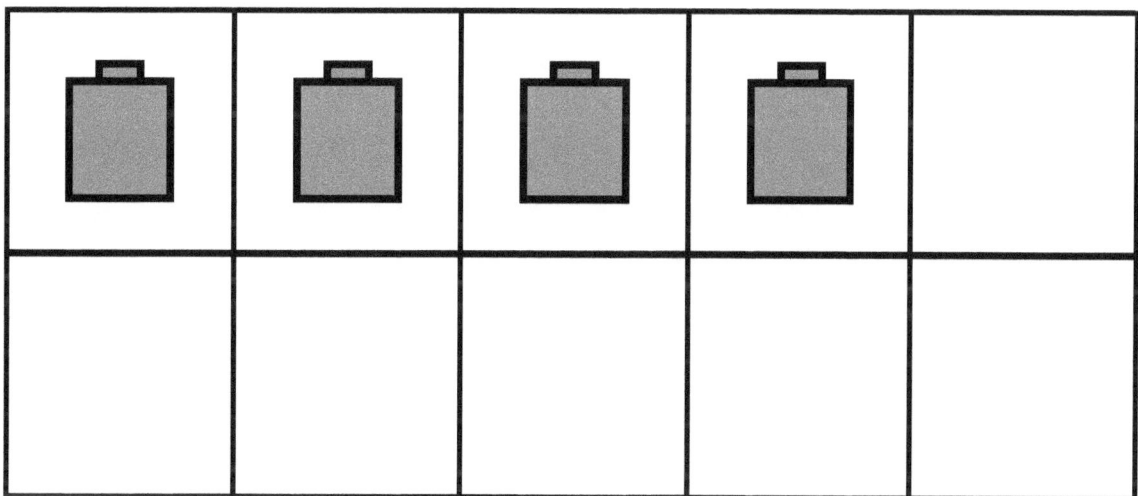

$$10 + \boxed{} = 10$$

- -

How many more cubes do you need to make 10?

$$4 + \boxed{} = 10$$

How many more cubes do you need to make 10?

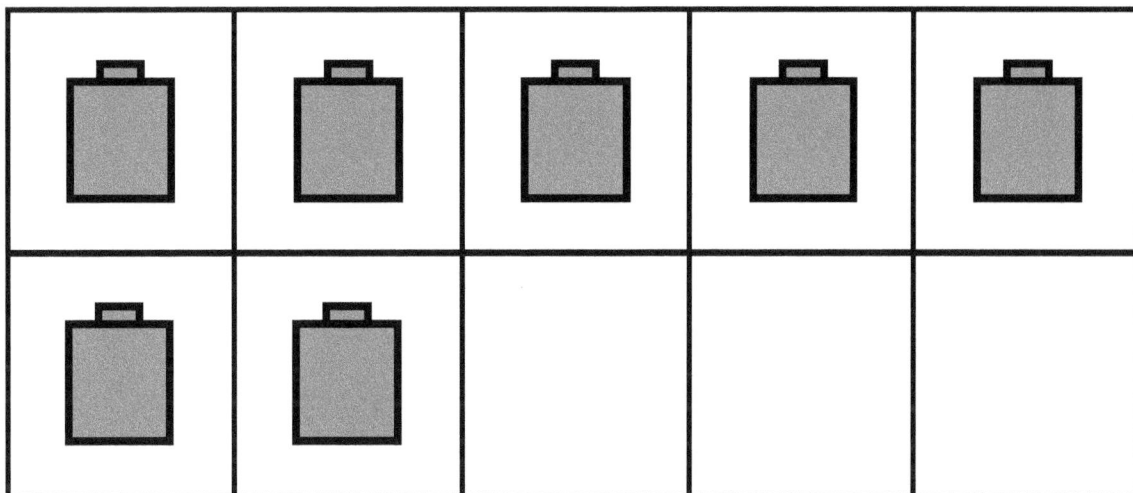

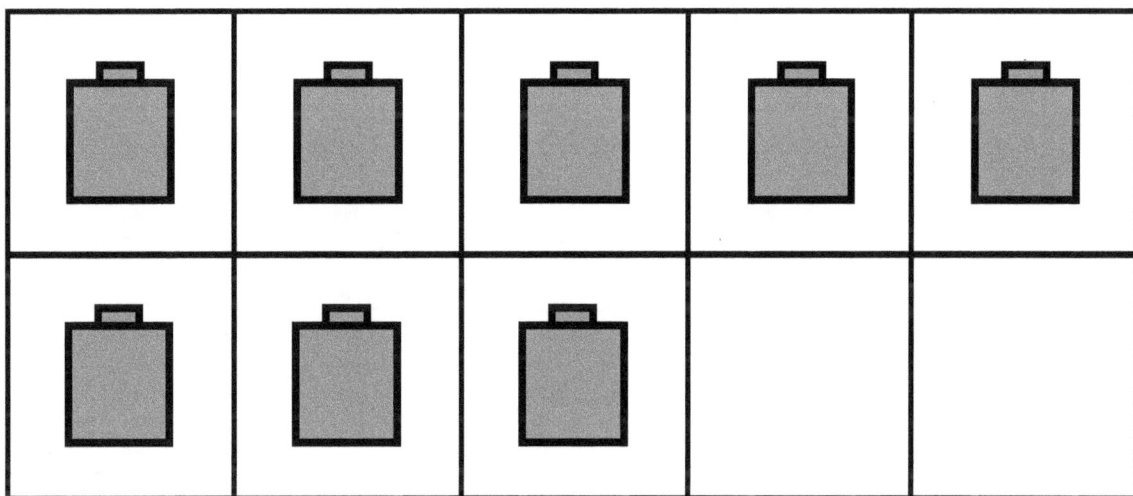

$$7 + \boxed{} = 10$$

- -

How many more cubes do you need to make 10?

$$8 + \boxed{} = 10$$

How many more cubes do you need to make 10?

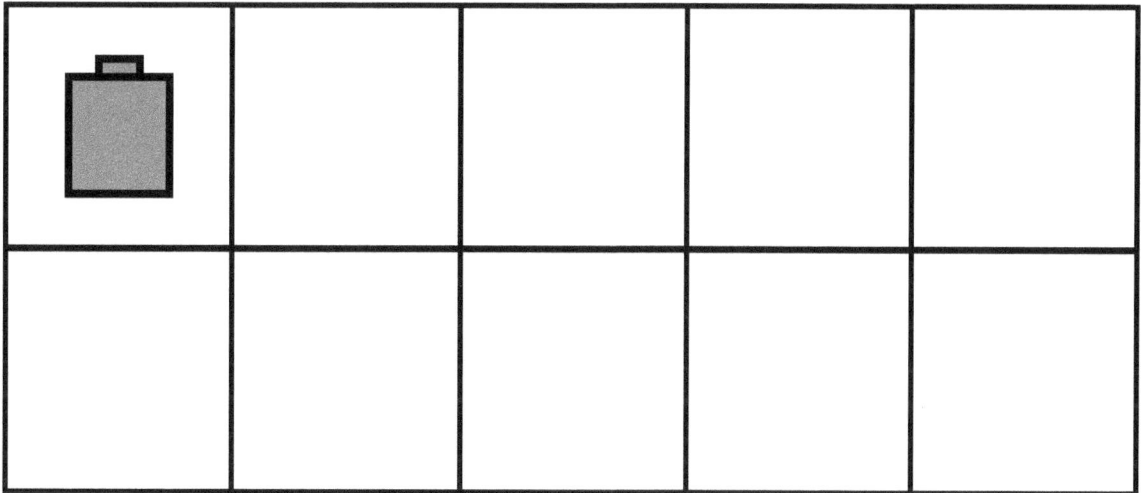

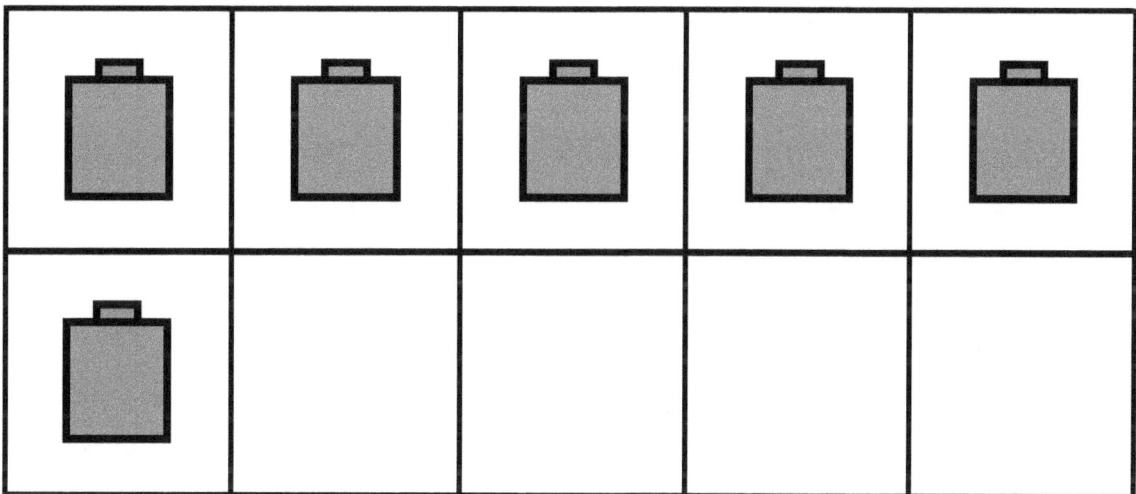

$$1 + \boxed{} = 10$$

- -

How many more cubes do you need to make 10?

$$6 + \boxed{} = 10$$

How many more cubes do you need to make 10?

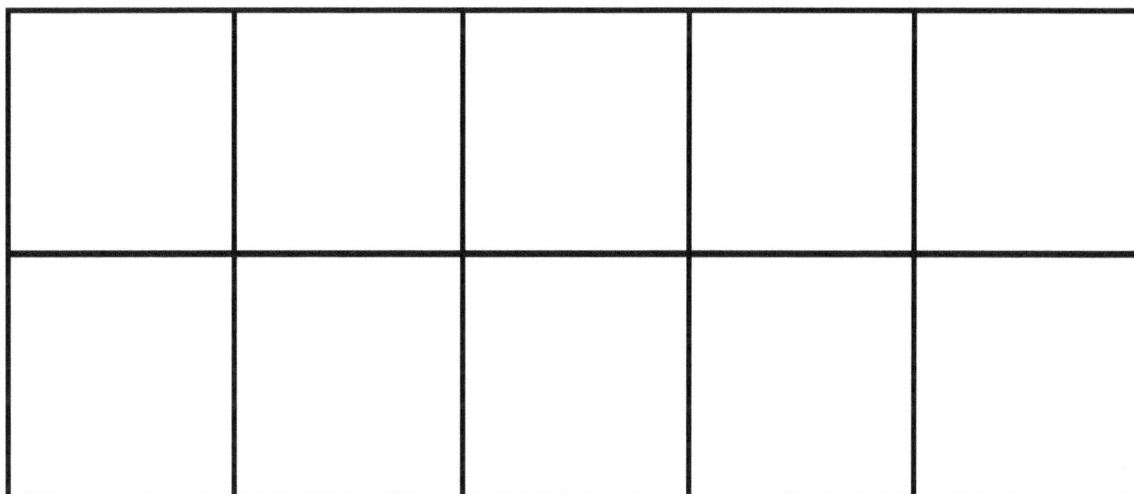

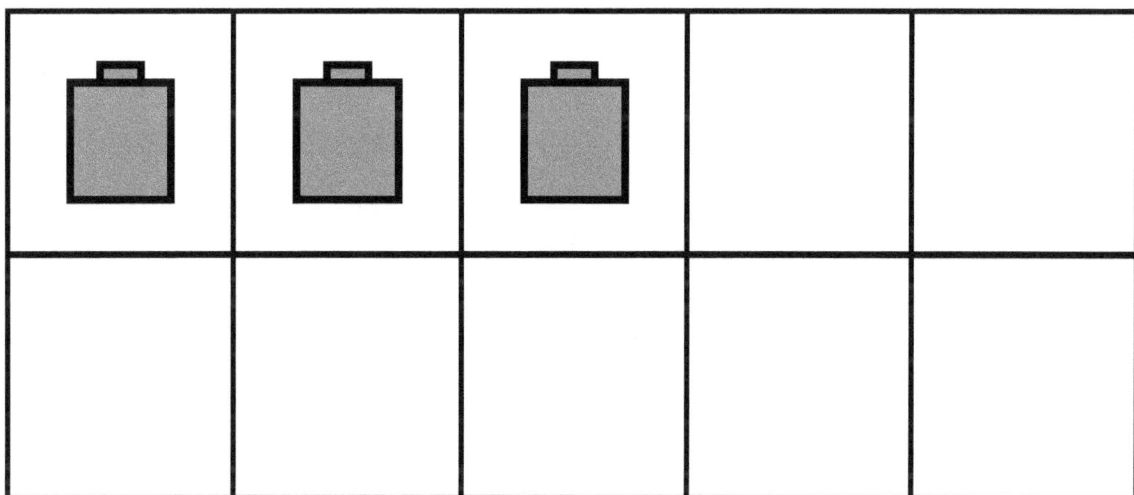

$$0 + \boxed{} = 10$$

- -

How many more cubes do you need to make 10?

$$3 + \boxed{} = 10$$

How many more cubes do you need to make 10?

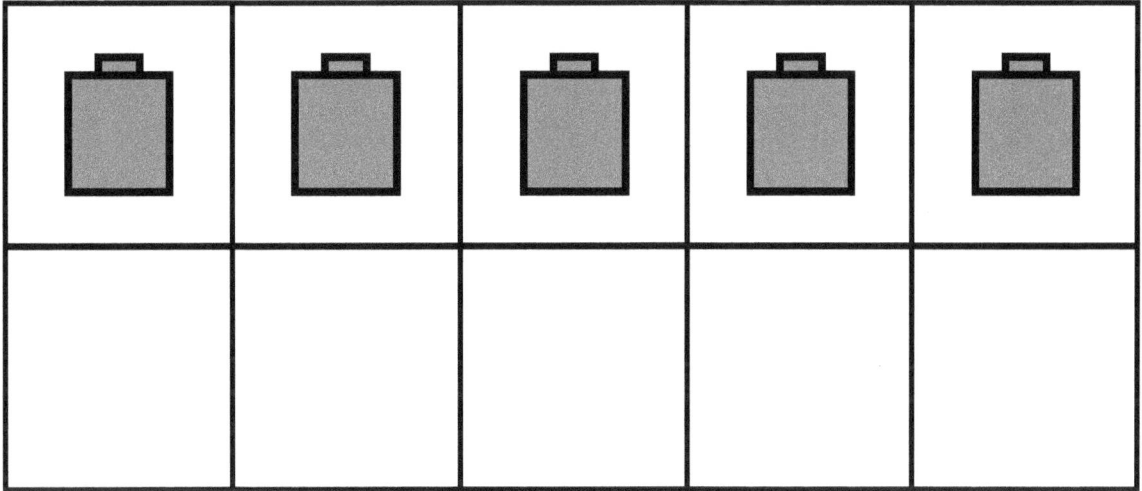

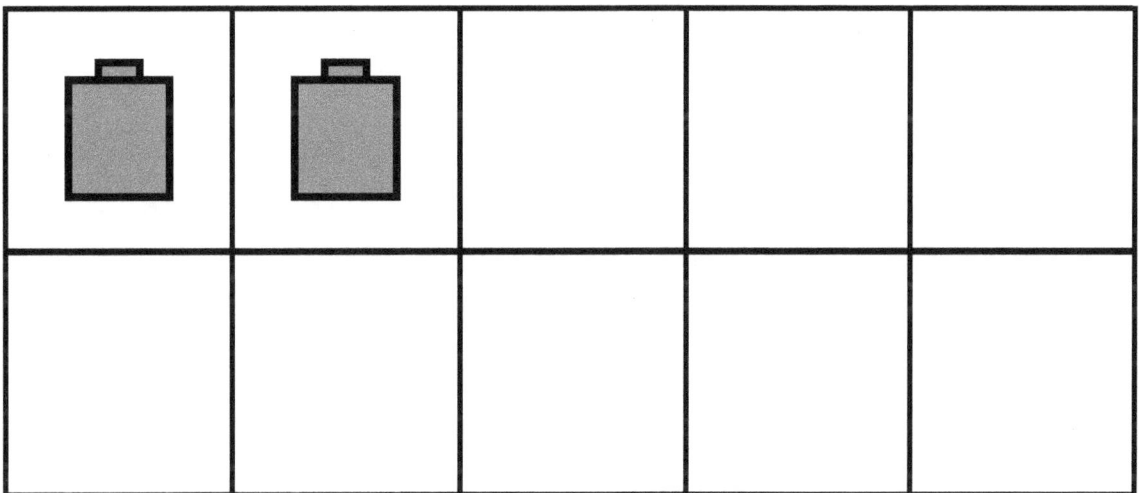

$$5 + \boxed{} = 10$$

How many more cubes do you need to make 10?

$$2 + \boxed{} = 10$$

Hop to the Finish!
-THE ADDITION VERSION-

KEY CONCEPT

Adding within 10 on a number line

PLAYERS

2 players

MATERIALS

- *Hop to the Finish addition gameboard.* Two students can share the same gameboard, which helps them to compare their numbers and see which player has the higher number. Alternatively, you can cut out player one and player two's gameboard so that each student has their own gameboard. You can laminate the gameboards to last longer.
- *Spinner.* You can use the provided spinner by attaching the arrow to the spinner with a paper fastener. Alternatively, you can use a dice with small numbers or students can pull cards with the numbers 0, 1, and 2.
- *Game pieces* (not provided). You can use game pieces from another classroom game, or small counters.

DIRECTIONS

1. Every player starts on zero.
2. Player one spins the spinner. The number player one lands on tells him or her how many spaces to move the game piece to the right.
3. Player two spins the spinner. The number player two lands on tells him or her how many spaces to move the game piece to the right.
4. The players continue to take turns spinning the spinner and moving their game pieces to the right. The first player to make it to 10 wins!

Player One:

0 1 2 3 4 5 6 7 8 9 10

start → finish!

Player Two:

0 1 2 3 4 5 6 7 8 9 10

start → finish!

Hop to the Finish!
-THE SUBTRACTION VERSION-

KEY CONCEPT
Subtracting within 10 on a number line

PLAYERS

2 players

MATERIALS

- *Hop to the Finish subtraction gameboard.* Two students can share the same gameboard, which helps them to compare their numbers and see which player has the lower number. Alternatively, you can cut out player one and player two's gameboard so that each student has their own gameboard. You can laminate the gameboards to last longer.
- *Spinner.* You can use the provided spinner by attaching the arrow to the spinner with a paper fastener. Alternatively, you can use a dice with small numbers or students can pull cards with the numbers 0, 1, and 2.
- *Game pieces* (not provided). You can use game pieces from another classroom game, or small counters.

DIRECTIONS

1. Every player starts on 10 on the right side of the board.
2. Player one spins the spinner. The number player one lands on tells him or her how many spaces to move the game piece to the left.
3. Player two spins the spinner. The number player two lands on tells him or her how many spaces to move the game piece to the left.
4. The players continue to take turns spinning the spinner and moving their game pieces to the left. The first player to make it to 0 wins!

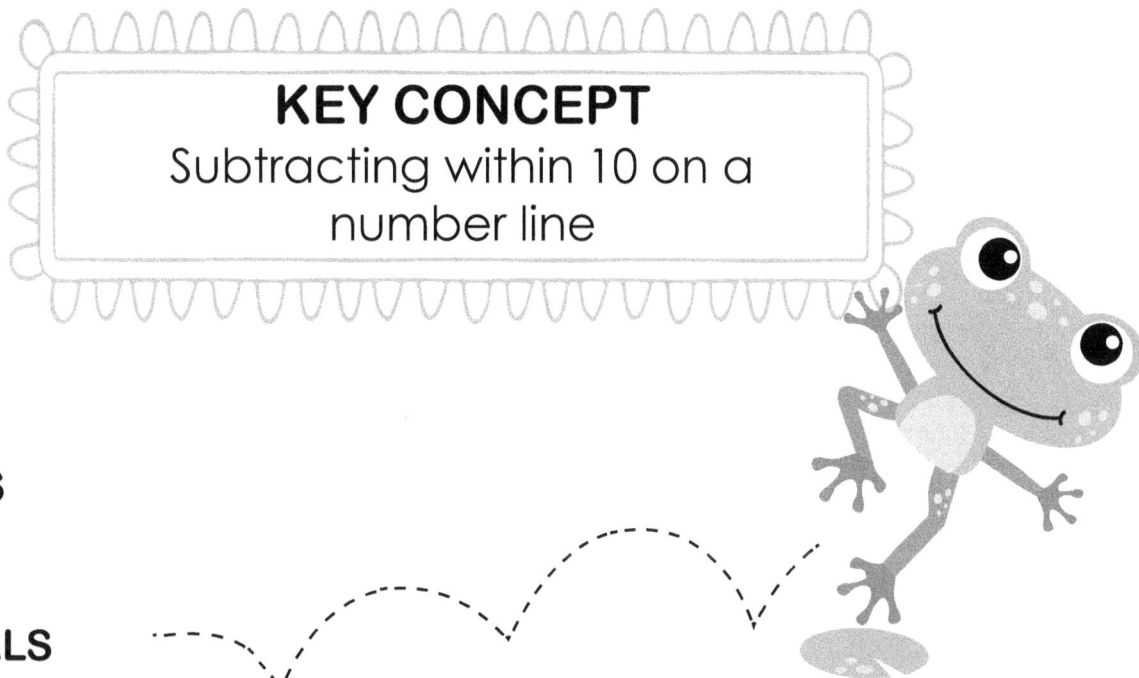

Player One:

start →

finish!

Player Two:

start →

finish!

Hop to the Finish!
-SPINNER-

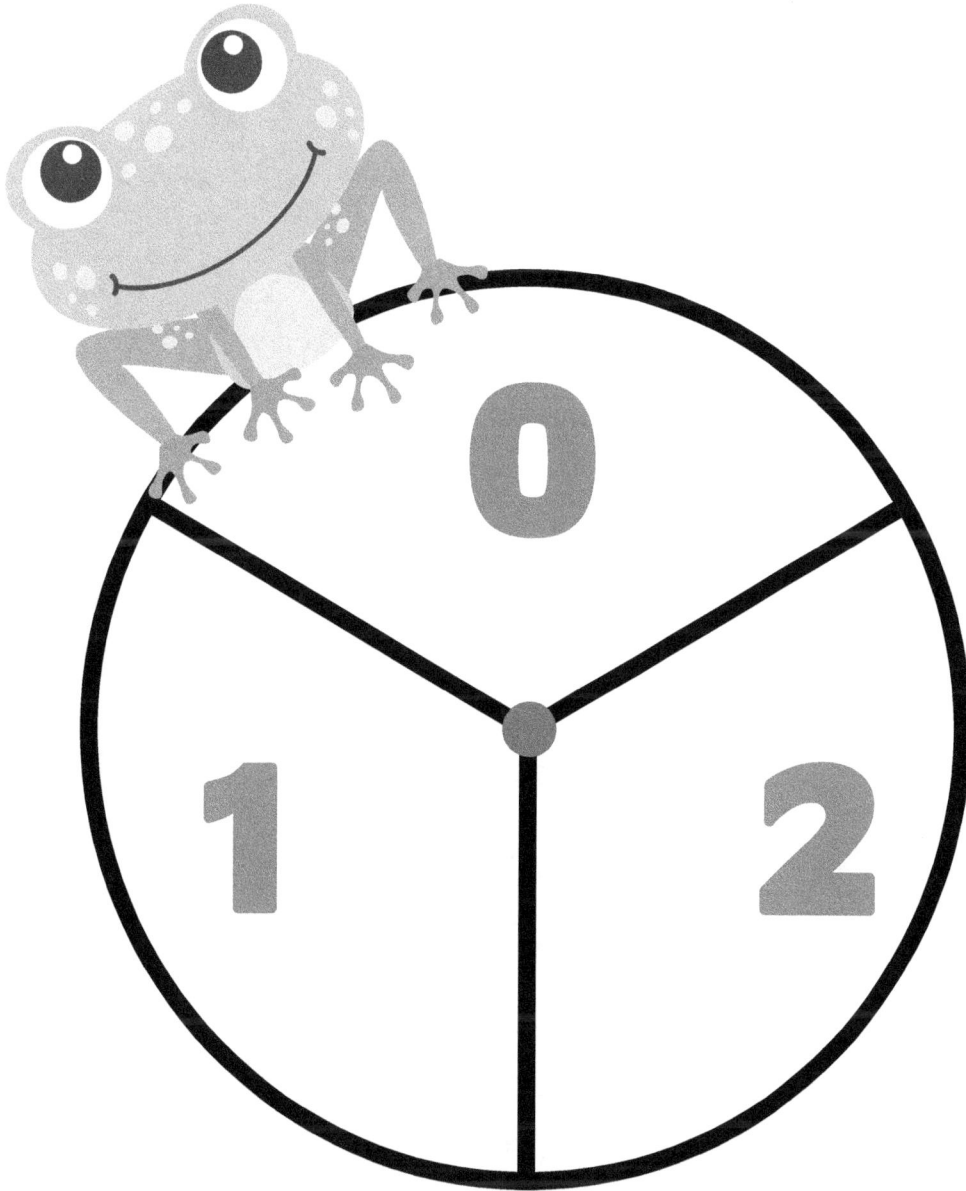

0

1

2

www.luminouslearning.com

Directions for assembling the spinner:
1. Cut on the dotted lines above to separate the spinner.
2. Cut out the arrow.
3. Attach the arrow to the center of the spinner using a paper fastener.

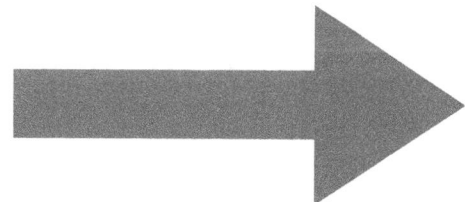

Subtract 'em

SMALL GROUP ACTIVITY

1 - 6 students

MATERIALS

- *Subtract 'em cards.* There are 36 cards that each have a different equation written on it. Cut out each card along the dotted lines. You can laminate the cards so that they last longer.
- *Dry erase marker* (optional). If you laminate the cards, students can use a dry erase marker to cross out the number of cubes indicated in the equation. Otherwise, students can cross them out using a pencil.

DIRECTIONS

1. The student takes a card and reads the equation written on the card.
2. The student crosses out the number of unifix cubes indicated by the equation. For example, if the card reads 8 - 6, the student crosses off 6 unifix cubes.

3. The student counts the remaining number of unifix cubes to find the difference of the equation. For example, 8 - 6 = ⬚2⬚. If the cards are laminated, the student can fill in the difference on the card. Otherwise, students can write the difference using a pencil.
4. The student continues to take cards and repeats steps 1 - 3.

6 - 1 =

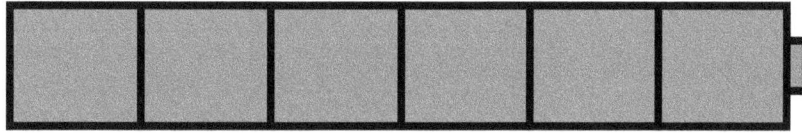

5 - 3 =

7 - 4 =

10 - 5 = ☐

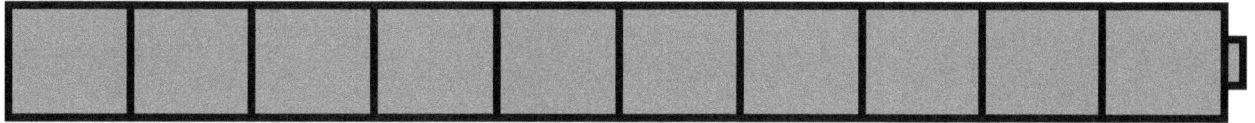

8 - 4 = ☐

9 - 2 = ☐

6 - 4 =

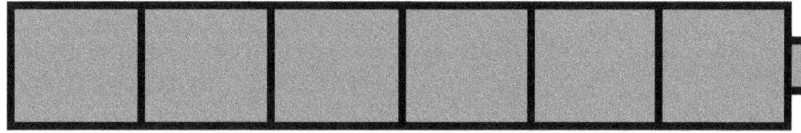

7 - 1 =

4 - 2 =

9 - 5 =

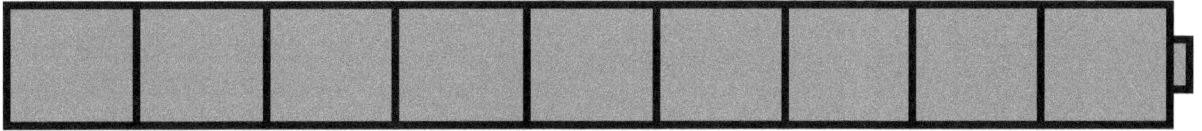

3 - 2 =

9 - 3 =

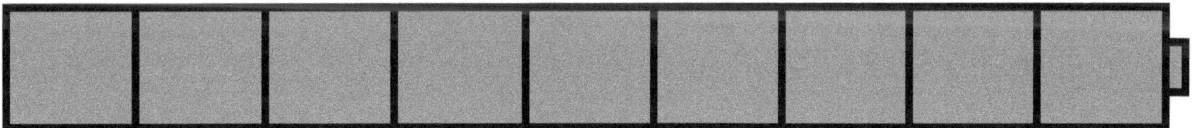

8 - 2 = ☐

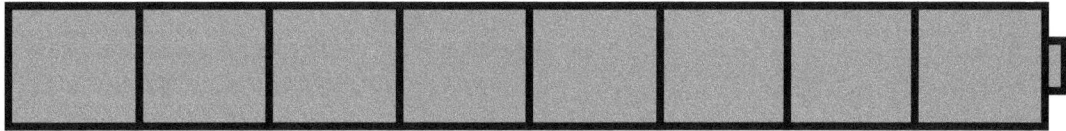

5 - 1 = ☐

4 - 4 = ☐

8 - 6 =

9 - 7 =

7 - 6 =

4 - 3 =

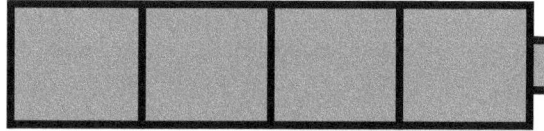

6 - 3 =

7 - 3 =

9 - 6 =

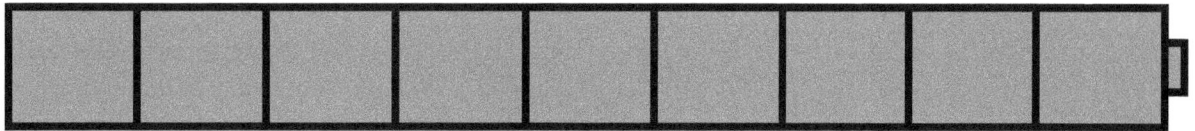

8 - 5 =

10 - 3 =

7 - 7 =

8 - 3 =

9 - 8 =

7 - 5 =

6 - 2 =

5 - 2 =

10 - 6 = ☐

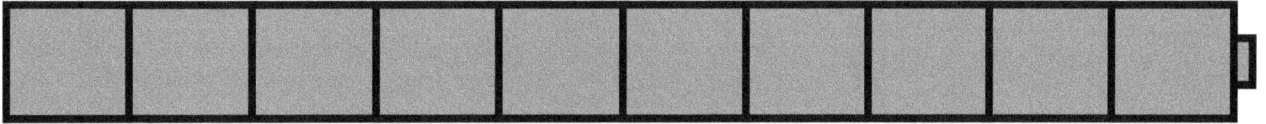

8 - 7 = ☐

6 - 6 = ☐

9 - 4 = ☐

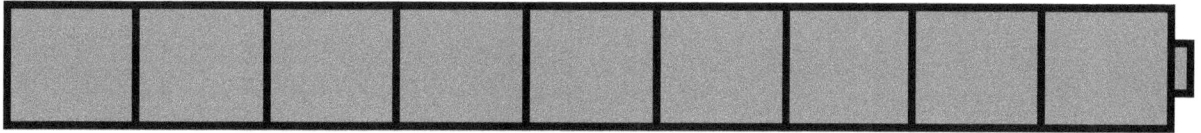

7 - 2 = ☐

5 - 4 = ☐

Add 'em up

SMALL GROUP ACTIVITY

1 - 6 students

MATERIALS

- *Add 'em up cards.* There are 48 cards that each have a different equation written on it. Cut out each card along the dotted lines. You can laminate the cards so that they last longer.

  *The cards progress in difficulty. The first 24 cards involve adding within 10. The second 24 cards involve adding within 20.

- *Unifix cubes.* Each student should have a basket of unifix cubes or other counters. Students will add the unifix cubes to find the sum.

- *Dry erase marker* (optional). If you laminate the cards, students can use a dry erase marker to fill in the equation when they determine the sum based on the equation on each card.

DIRECTIONS

1. The student takes a card and reads the equation written on the card.
2. The student puts together unifix cubes or counters based on the equation. *For example:* If the card reads 2 + 6, the student first takes 2 unifix cubes and then adds 6 more unifix cubes onto the stack.

3. The student adds all of the unifix cubes in the stack to find the sum. The student writes the answer in the blank on the card. If the cards are laminated, the student can fill in the sum using a dry erase marker.
4. The student continues to take cards and repeats steps 1 - 3.
5. Students can keep track of their sums and add the sums after they have gone through all the cards. The student with the greatest sum wins!

$$4 + 2 = \boxed{}$$

$$6 + 0 = \boxed{}$$

$$2 + 2 = \boxed{}$$

$$1 + 4 = \boxed{}$$

$$5 + 2 = \boxed{}$$

$$3 + 3 = \boxed{}$$

$$1 + 5 = \boxed{}$$

$$4 + 5 = \boxed{}$$

$$6 + 4 = \boxed{}$$

$$4 + 4 = \boxed{}$$

$$6 + 1 = \boxed{}$$

$$2 + 4 = \boxed{}$$

$$3 + 1 = \boxed{}$$

$$7 + 2 = \boxed{}$$

$$0 + 3 = \boxed{}$$

5 + 5 =

6 + 2 =

3 + 4 =

$$1 + 7 = \boxed{}$$

$$8 + 2 = \boxed{}$$

$$1 + 8 = \boxed{}$$

2 + 5 = ☐

4 + 3 = ☐

1 + 6 = ☐

7 + 4 =

9 + 5 =

8 + 3 =

$$5 + 8 = \boxed{}$$

$$11 + 2 = \boxed{}$$

$$14 + 3 = \boxed{}$$

4 + 10 = ☐

6 + 7 = ☐

7 + 7 = ☐

7 + 4 = ☐

6 + 9 = ☐

8 + 8 = ☐

15 + 2 = ☐

10 + 7 = ☐

9 + 9 = ☐

$$4 + 9 = \boxed{}$$

$$8 + 7 = \boxed{}$$

$$4 + 12 = \boxed{}$$

1 + 17 =

11 + 5 =

12 + 3 =

10 + 10 = ▢

5 + 10 = ▢

16 + 4 = ▢

All Aboard!
-THE ADDITION VERSION-

KEY CONCEPT

Adding within 20 on a number line

PLAYERS

2 players

MATERIALS

- *All Aboard addition gameboard (x2)*. Cut out and use the two gameboards, which will help students see which player has the higher number. Each student should write their name on the top of the gameboard. You can laminate the gameboards to last longer.
- *Spinner.* You can use the provided spinner by attaching the arrow to the spinner with a paper fastener. Alternatively, you can use a dice with small numbers or students can pull cards with the numbers 0, 1, 2, and 3.
- *Game pieces* (not provided). You can use game pieces from another classroom game, or small counters. Students will move these game pieces along the board as they play.

DIRECTIONS

1. Every player starts on zero.
2. Player one spins the spinner. The number player one lands on tells him or her how many spaces to move the game piece.
3. Player two spins the spinner. The number player two lands on tells him or her how many spaces to move the game piece.
4. The players continue to take turns spinning the spinner and moving their game pieces. The first player to make it to 20 wins!

Player One:

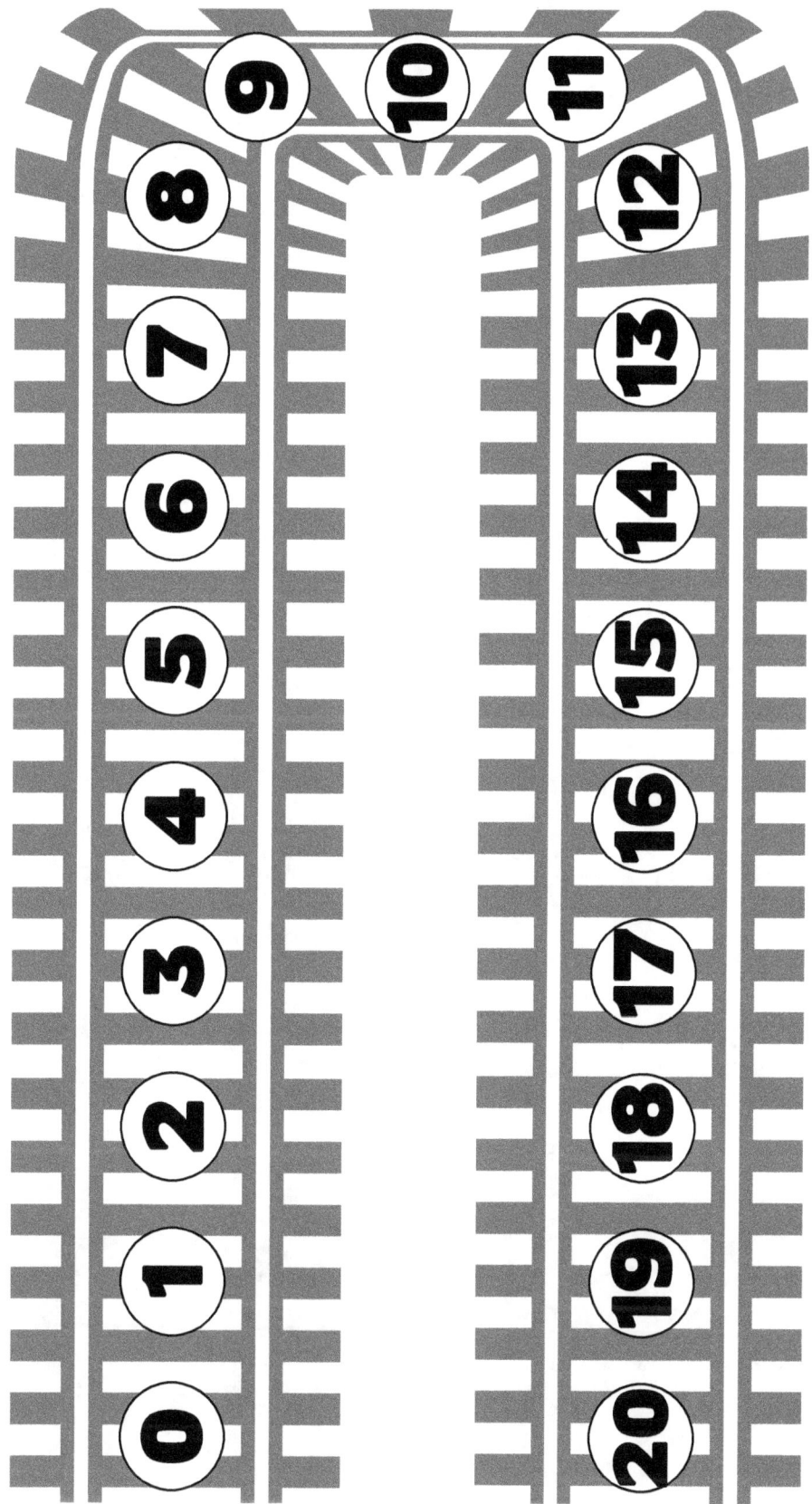

start

finish!

Player Two:

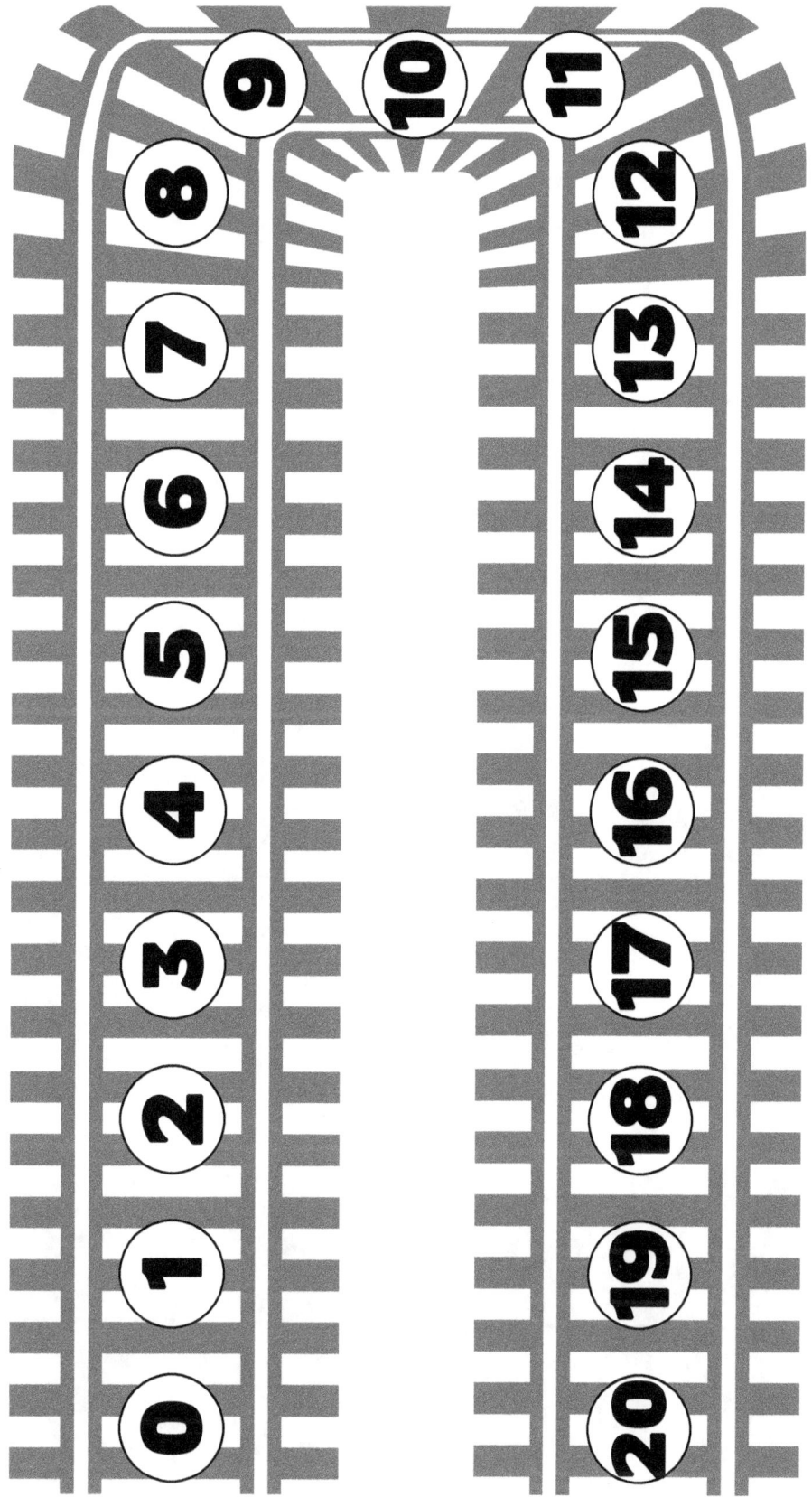

start

0 1 2 3 4 5 6 7 8 9 10 11 12 13 14 15 16 17 18 19 20

finish!

All Aboard!
-THE SUBTRACTION VERSION-

KEY CONCEPT
Subtracting within 20 on a number line

PLAYERS

2 players

MATERIALS

- *All Aboard subtraction gameboard (x2).* Cut out and use the two game-boards, which will help students see which player has the lower number. Each student should write their name on the top of the gameboard. You can laminate the gameboards to last longer.
- *Spinner.* You can use the provided spinner by attaching the arrow to the spinner with a paper fastener. Alternatively, you can use a dice with small numbers or students can pull cards with the numbers 0, 1, 2, and 3.
- *Game pieces* (not provided). You can use game pieces from another classroom game, or small counters. Students will move these game pieces along the board as they play.

DIRECTIONS

1. Every player starts on 20.
2. Player one spins the spinner. The number player one lands on tells him or her how many spaces to move the game piece.
3. Player two spins the spinner. The number player two lands on tells him or her how many spaces to move the game piece.
4. The players continue to take turns spinning the spinner and moving their game pieces. The first player to make it to 0 wins!

Player One:

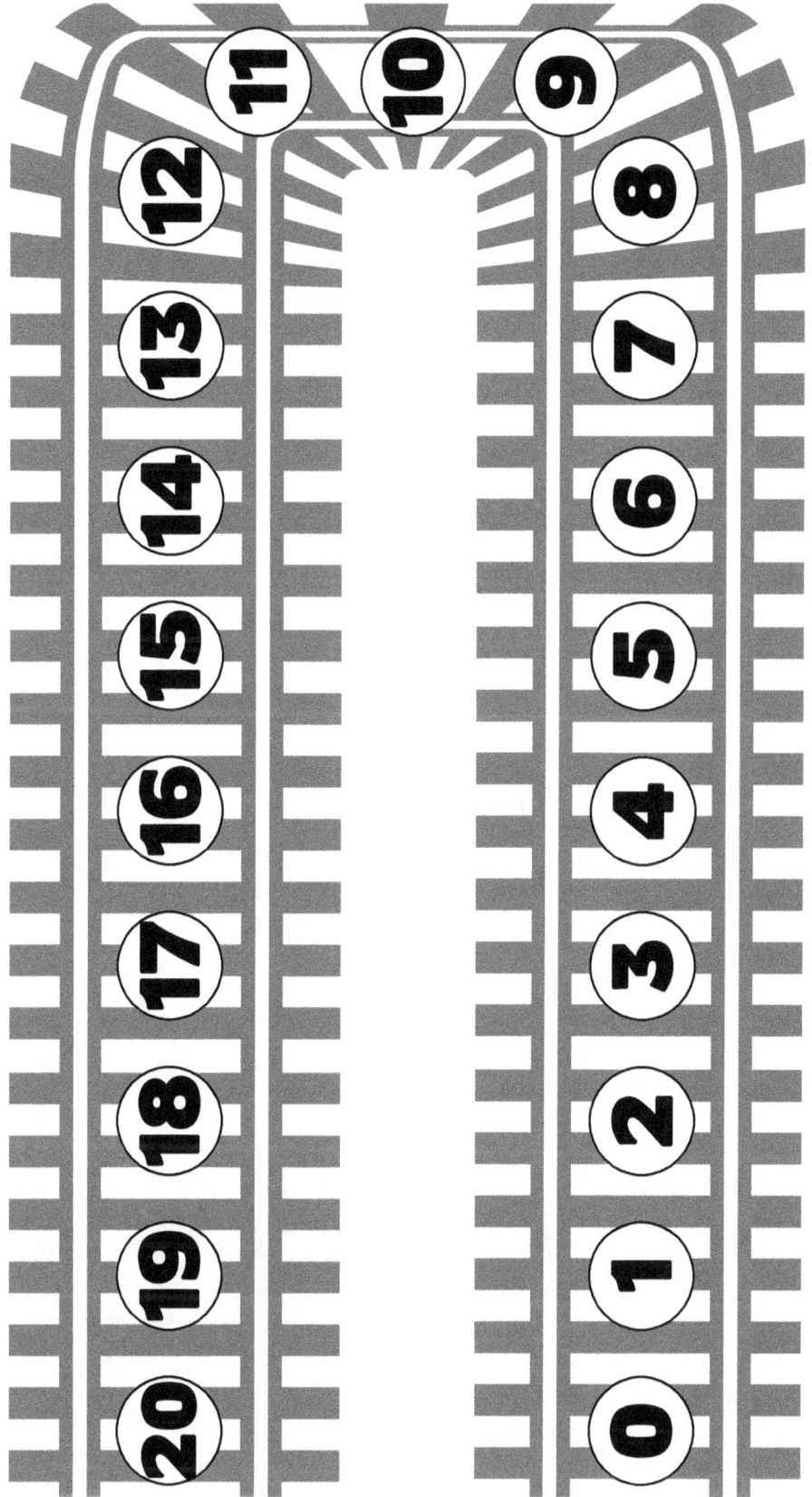

start

11 10 9

12 8

13 7

14 6

15 5

16 4

17 3

18 2

19 1

20 0

finish!

Player Two: _____

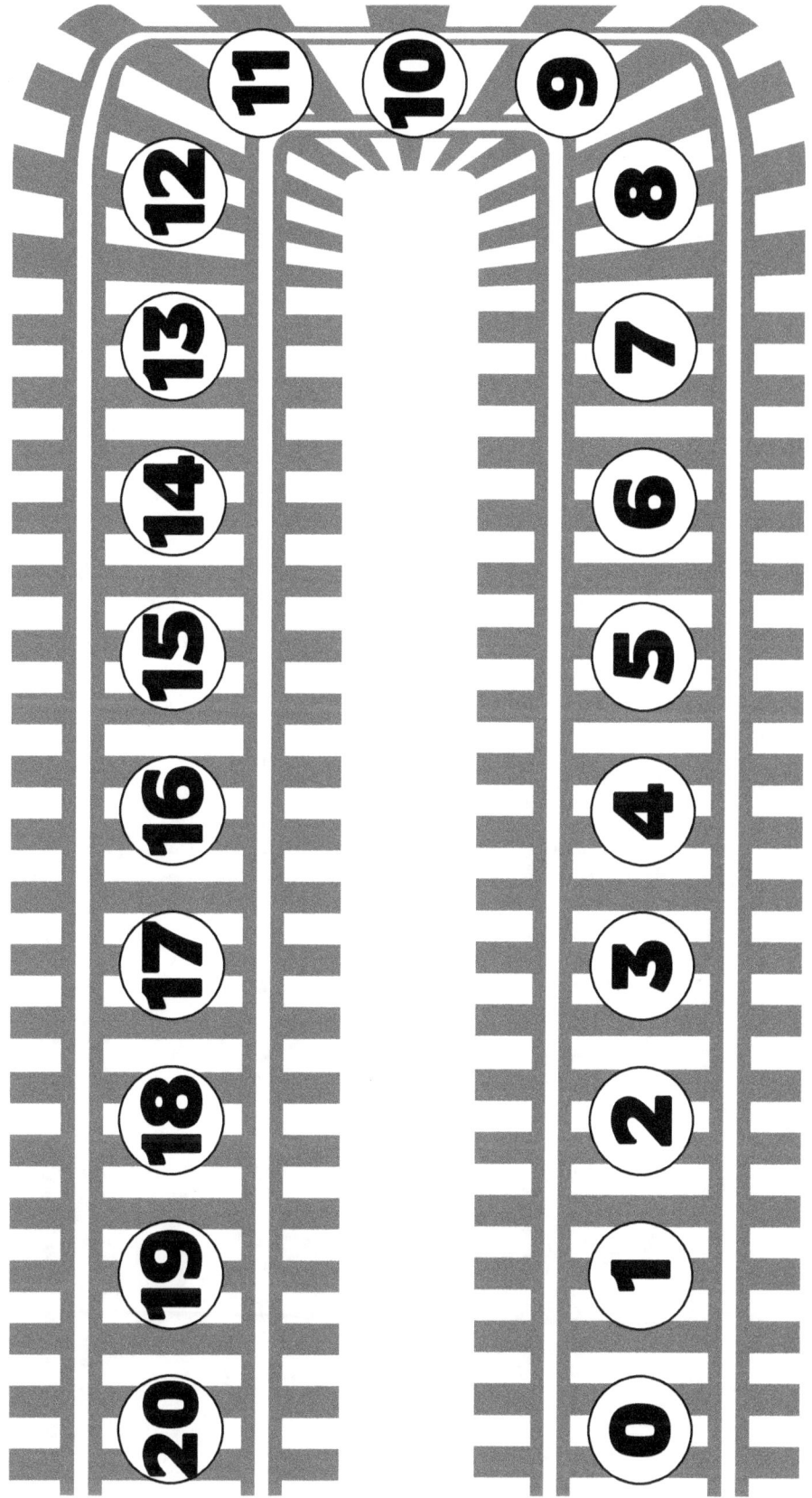

start

20 19 18 17 16 15 14 13 12 11 10 9 8 7 6 5 4 3 2 1 0

finish!

All Aboard!
-SPINNER-

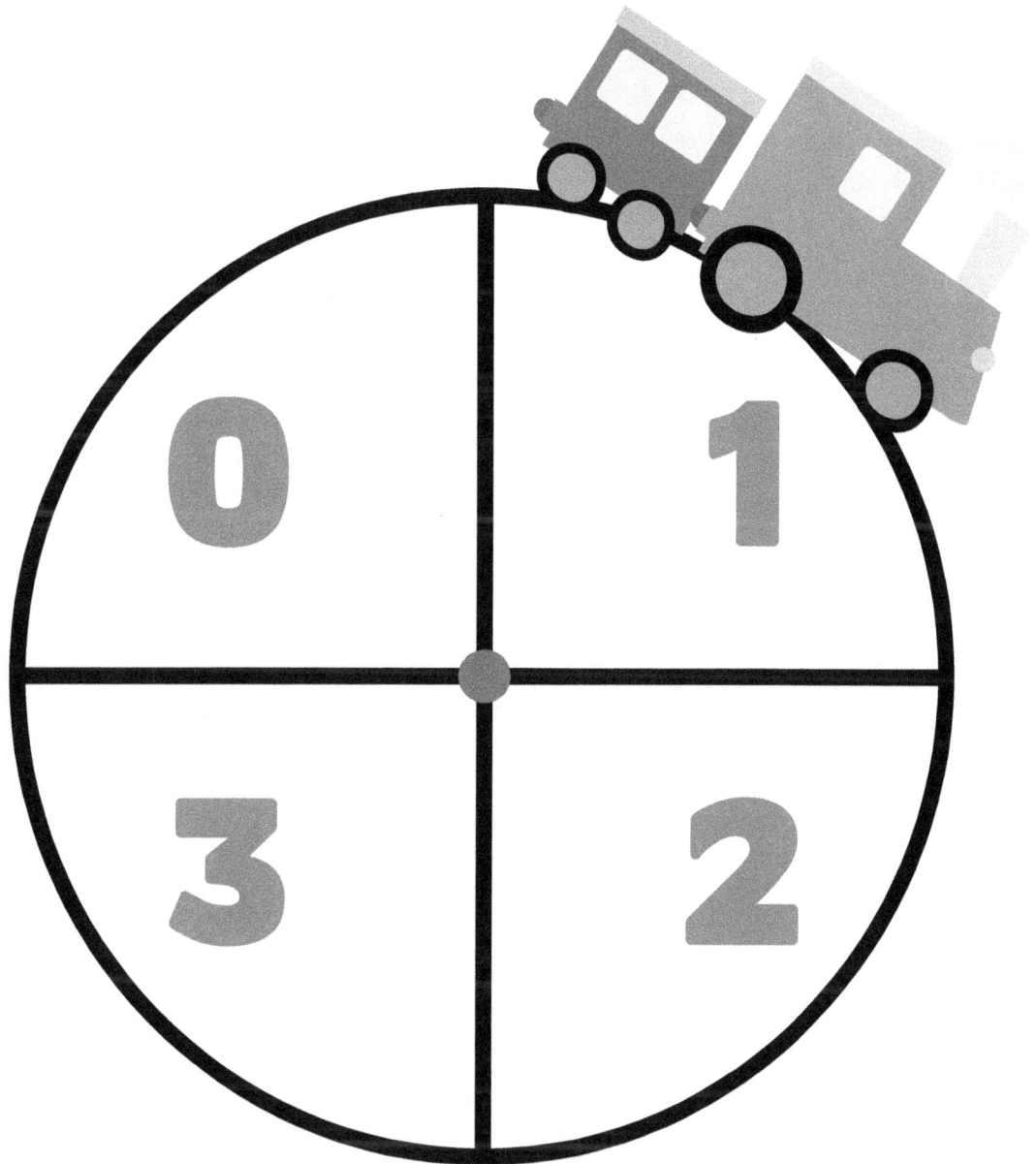

0   1

3   2

Directions for assembling the spinner:
1. Cut on the dotted lines above to separate the spinner.
2. Cut out the arrow.
3. Attach the arrow to the center of the spinner using a paper fastener.

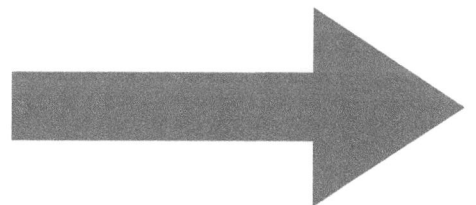

APPENDIX

Square tiles you can cut out and use instead of unifix cubes

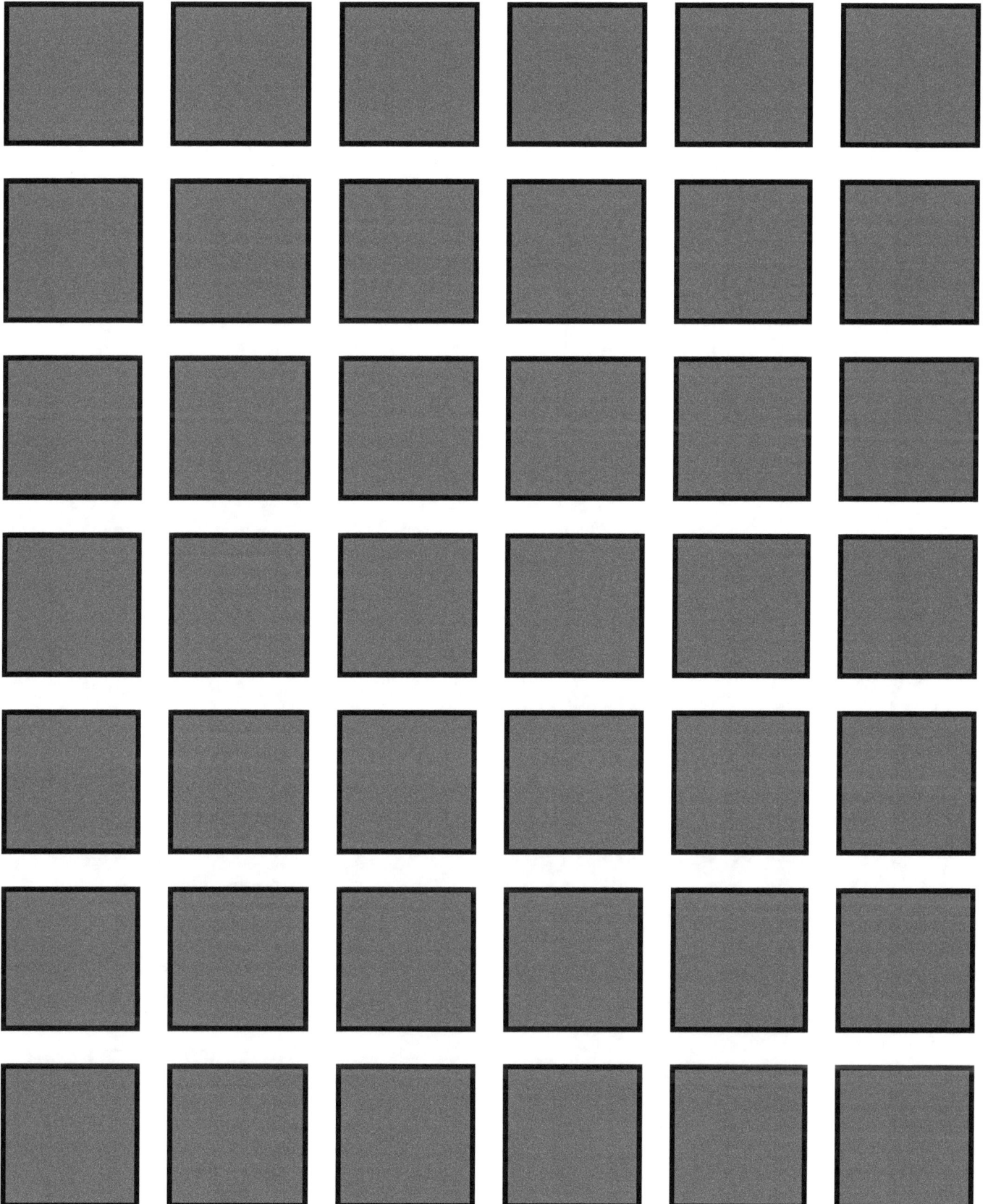

APPENDIX

Square tiles you can cut out and use instead of unifix cubes

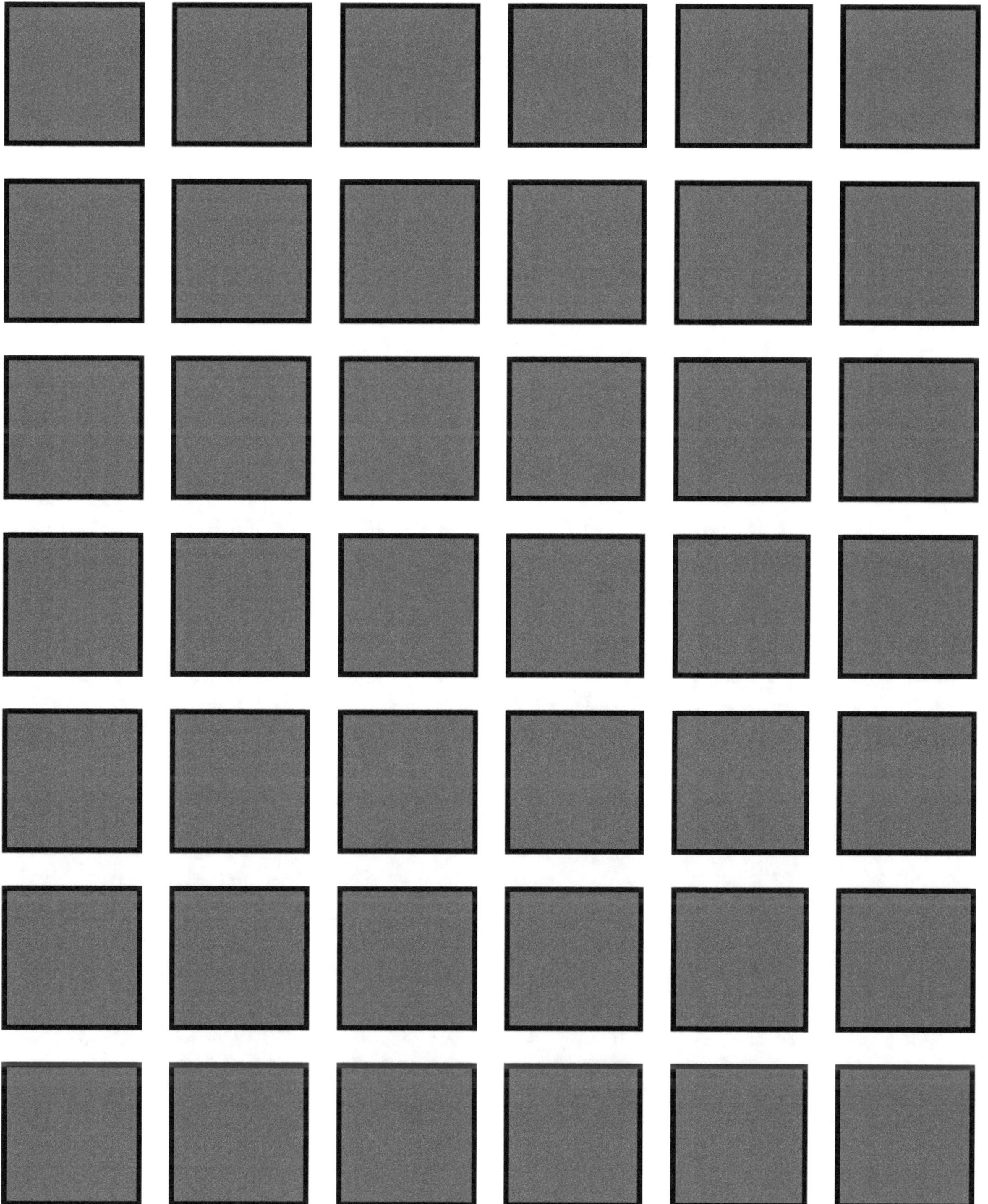

www.ingramcontent.com/pod-product-compliance
Lightning Source LLC
LaVergne TN
LVHW081346060426
835508LV00017B/1444